CONTENTS

Evolution

Animals

Humans

Some words are shown in bold, **like this**. You can find out what they mean by looking in the glossary.

Everywhere you look, Earth is full of life. From humans, crocodiles and ostriches to trees, mushrooms and even creepy slime moulds, life comes in all shapes and sizes. But where did all these weird and wonderful **organisms** come from? Have they always been here?

The variety of life on Earth is simply amazing.

WAY BACK WHEN

Billions of years ago, when the planet was young, there was nothing living on it. But eventually, different chemicals randomly grouped together into **molecules**. The molecules could make copies of themselves. And that was just the beginning. Ever since then, the **cells** that make up organisms have continued to make copies of themselves. Over millions of years, they have branched off into different types of life. The name for this process? Evolution!

HAIRY PAST

Evolution and Life on Earth

Nancy Dickmann

raintree 🍃

a Capstone company — publishers for

Raintree is an imprint of Capstone Global Library Limited, a company incorporated in England and Wales having its registered office at 264 Banbury Road, Oxford, OX2 7DY – Registered company number: 6695582

www.raintree.co.uk
myorders@raintree.co.uk

Edited by Helen Cox Cannons
Designed by Philippa Jenkins (cover) and Charmaine Whitman (interior)
Picture research by Morgan Walters
Production by Tori Abraham
Originated by Capstone Global Library Limited
Printed and bound in India

ISBN 978 1 4747 5485 9 (hardback)
21 20 19 18 17
10 9 8 7 6 5 4 3 2 1

ISBN 978 1 4747 5487 3 (paperback)
22 21 20 19
10 9 8 7 6 5 4 3 2 1

British Library Cataloguing in Publication Data
A full catalogue record for this book is available from the British Library.

Acknowledgements
The publishers and author would like to thank May Lewis (aged 10) and Imogen Gilbert (aged 9) for the drawings on page 44.

The publishers would also like to thank Michael Bright for his invaluable help in the preparation of this book.

We would like to thank the following for permission to reproduce photographs: Alamy: Iain Masterton, 32, Sabena Jane Blackbird, 30, Science Picture Co, 31; Capstone Press: John Hughs, 15; Getty Images: Auscape, top 25, Michael Ochs Archives, 40; iStockphoto: JohnCarnemolla, bottom 26, Pavliha, 36, Wlad74, 28; Science Source: NHM, 33; Shutterstock: A and N photography, top left 38, Abeselom Zerit, 17, Africa Studio, top middle left 39, Air Images, middle right 39, Amanda Carden, 8, Antonio Guillem, 35, Anukool Manoton, top 22, AuntSpray, (mammoth) cover, 1, 2, 3, Be Good, bottom right 39, Bildagentur Zoonar GmbH, (human vector) 29, Brian Eichhorn, bottom right 38, Catmando, (dinosaur) top right cover, 1, Chris Price at PulseFoto, bottom 11, Cookie Studio, middle left 39, Dancestrokes, bottom 24, Darren Whittingham, (hairy frame) design element throughout, Dennis W Donohue, top 18, Djomas, middle left 38, Donna Ellen Coleman, bottom left 38, Ethan Daniels, bottom 22, Freer, (dinosaur) bottom left cover, 1, Georgios Kollidas, 10, gkuna, (stones) Cover, Gregory Dean, top right 38, Harold Stiver, bottom 20, Harper 3D, (hairy letters) Cover, imagevixen, 6, Ivan Kuzmin, top 24, JT Platt, top 23, kelldallfall, bottom 21, Kzenon, 42, lanych, top middle 38, Lisa F. Young, top middle right 39, LouisLotterPhotography, bottom 18, manfredxy, (smoke) middle right 13, Marcio Jose Bastos Silva, top left 29, Martin Fowler, (white moth) 12, Martin Mecnarowski, bottom 25, michaeljung, top right 39, Mongolka, (birch) 12, 13, Monkey Business Images, 34, bottom middle 38, munalin, 41, NadzeyaShanchuk, (man, girl vector) 29, 40, Nick Biemans, (monkey) cover, 1, 2, ostill, bottom left 39, PixieMe, top left 39, Rainer Albiez, 5, Rawpixel.com, 37, Reinhold Leitner, bottom 23, Ricardo Saraiva, (face) cover, 1, 2, Roger Clark ARPS, top 27, Rost9, 3, 7, 41, S1001, (sunsuet) Cover, Sergey Uryadnikov, top 11, top 19, siriwat wongchana, (stone) design element, sisqopote, 9, Smit, (sky) design element, SrjT, 14, Standret, top 43, Steve McWilliam, (brown moth) 12, 13, szefei, bottom right 38, tristan tan, (forest) 16, Trueblackheart, bottom 27, Uwe Bergwitz, top 20, Vlad61, 4, Vladimir Mucibabic, (chest) cover, 1, 2, Warpaint, (dinosaur) middle cover, 1, (calfs) 16, Zynatis, bottom 43; SuperStock: Biosphoto, bottom 19, Cultura Limited, top 21, DeAgostini, 45, Pablo Méndez / age fotostock, top 26.

Every effort has been made to contact copyright holders of material reproduced in this book. Any omissions will be rectified in subsequent printings if notice is given to the publisher.

All the internet addresses (URLs) given in this book were valid at the time of going to press. However, due to the dynamic nature of the internet, some addresses may have changed, or sites may have changed or ceased to exist since publication. While the author and publisher regret any inconvenience this may cause readers, no responsibility for any such changes can be accepted by either the author or the publisher.

EVOLVE OR DIE

Evolution is the theory that all life forms that exist today developed from those first simple cells. First these life forms lived in water, then some moved onto land. Some learned to fly, and others to run. These changes came about because Earth was changing too. The **climate** has varied wildly over billions of years, from ice ages to floods and droughts. The landscape has changed as well. The living things that **adapted** to new conditions were more likely to survive.

By the numbers

Unidentified species

Each different type of organism is a **species**. Humans are a species, and so are pineapples. Scientists estimate that today there are about 8.7 million different species of plants, animals, fungi and other organisms. But scientists have only found and named about 1.2 million of them so far. There is a lot of work still to do!

Identified species

At times in the past, volcanic eruptions have changed Earth's climate and landscape.

HOW EVOLUTION WORKS

Evolution is a simple process, but it takes time. All living things produce **offspring**. These offspring are similar to their parents, but not exactly the same. They may eventually have their own offspring. Over a very long time, the tiny changes between parents and offspring can lead to some very large differences.

Parents and their children often look alike, but they are never identical.

PASS IT ON!

The colour of your hair, the shape of your ears, even the number of fingers you have – these are all **traits**. Traits are controlled by tiny units called **genes**. Genes are arranged into larger structures called **chromosomes**. Chromosomes are found in every cell, and they come in pairs. One of each pair came from your father, and the other from your mother.

Some versions of a gene are stronger, or more dominant, than others. For example, the gene for brown eyes is dominant over the gene for blue eyes. If you get a brown eye gene from your mother and a blue eye gene from your father, you will probably have brown eyes.

MUTANT ALERT!

Genes are made of strands of something called **DNA**. Sometimes an organism's DNA changes randomly – this is called **mutation**. A mutation may be harmful. If it is, the organism will probably die, and so will the mutation. But some mutations actually help the organism. They might make it better adapted to its **habitat**. This makes the organism more likely to survive. Any of its offspring with the same mutation will probably do well too. They will pass the mutation on to the next generation.

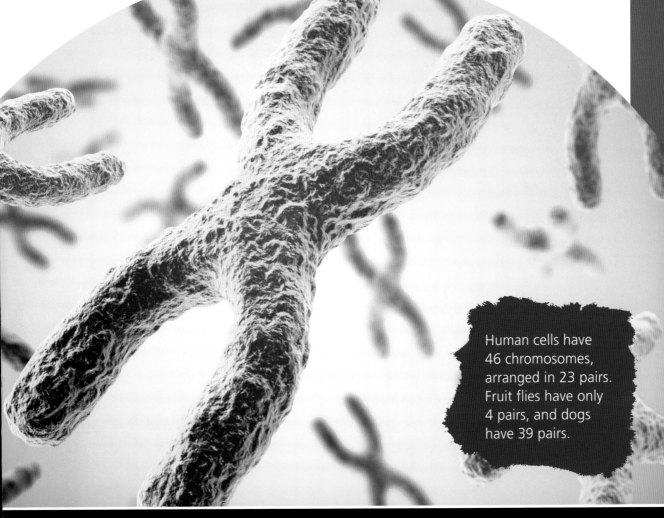

Human cells have 46 chromosomes, arranged in 23 pairs. Fruit flies have only 4 pairs, and dogs have 39 pairs.

DISCOVERING EVOLUTION

Evolution took a lot of working out. And in the meantime, there were a lot of ideas floating around!

WHERE DID WE COME FROM?

Different **cultures** have different ideas about where life came from. Some people believe that gods or spirits created the world. And if you believe that, it's harder to accept the idea that some **species** die out and new ones **evolve**. Why? Because that would suggest that the god who created everything didn't get it quite right.

Evolution is still controversial for some, though many accept the idea of evolution alongside their belief in gods or spirits.

Some Christians thought fossils were the bones of animals who didn't get onto Noah's Ark, and drowned during the flood described in the Bible.

By the numbers

In 1650, an Irish bishop, James Ussher, thought he could work out the date that Earth was created by adding up the ages of people mentioned in the Bible. His final answer was Sunday 23 October 4004 BC. He was out by about 4.5 billion years!

MYSTERIOUS BONES

People who believe that God created the world are called creationists. In the 18th century, their ideas kept coming up against the same problem: **fossils**. For centuries people had discovered fossils of **extinct** creatures, including dinosaurs. Some people explained them away by saying that these creatures must still be alive, just hiding in remote, unexplored areas.

But people found more and more fossils. A woman called Mary Anning (1799–1847), who searched the cliffs of Lyme Regis, found bizarre creatures such as plesiosaurs and ichthyosaurs. These bones clearly weren't from any animals that were living today.

Anning's discoveries supported the idea that many types of creatures were now extinct.

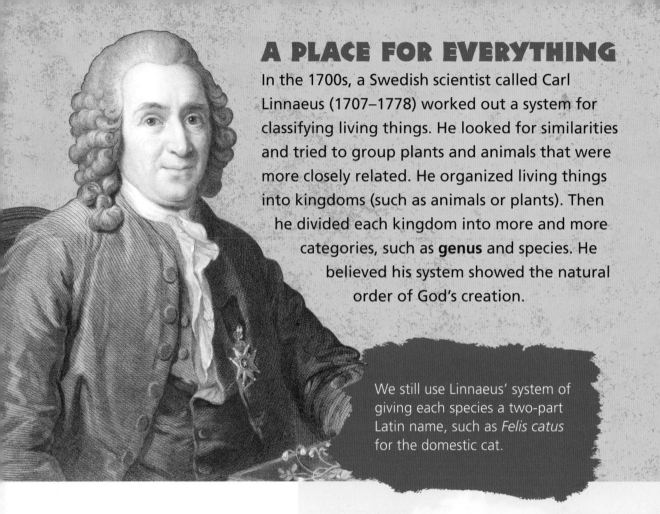

A PLACE FOR EVERYTHING

In the 1700s, a Swedish scientist called Carl Linnaeus (1707–1778) worked out a system for classifying living things. He looked for similarities and tried to group plants and animals that were more closely related. He organized living things into kingdoms (such as animals or plants). Then he divided each kingdom into more and more categories, such as **genus** and species. He believed his system showed the natural order of God's creation.

We still use Linnaeus' system of giving each species a two-part Latin name, such as *Felis catus* for the domestic cat.

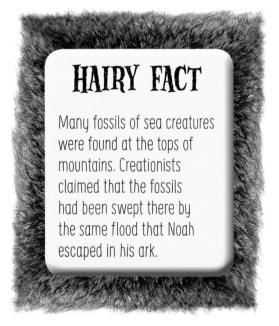

HAIRY FACT

Many fossils of sea creatures were found at the tops of mountains. Creationists claimed that the fossils had been swept there by the same flood that Noah escaped in his ark.

ALL CHANGE?

In the 1800s, another scientist tried to explain how living things change. Jean-Baptiste Lamarck (1744–1829) thought that an animal's body could change shape during its lifetime. For example, if a giraffe had to stretch to reach high leaves, its neck would grow. It would then pass this longer neck onto its **offspring**. This was wrong, but it did introduce the idea that species could change over time.

BUT WAIT A MINUTE...

The fact that it was scientifically impossible wasn't the only problem with Lamarck's theory. It also went against the idea that God had created all species exactly as they appear now. Conflict between the evolutionists and the creationists was coming to a head. After all, they couldn't both be right!

According to Lamarck, penguins have small wings because they did not use them to fly, so the wings shrank. We now know this isn't true.

DARWIN'S BIG IDEA

Charles Darwin (1809–1882) was a **naturalist**. He noticed that tortoises in the Galápagos Islands were slightly different from one island to the next. This led to his theory of **natural selection**.

Darwin's big idea was that within any species there will be some **variation**. Some individuals might be bigger, or a different colour. If a variation makes an **organism** better adapted to its **habitat**, it is more likely to survive. Then it passes its **traits** on to its offspring. Over time, this might result in a new species.

NATURAL SELECTION IN ACTION

1 The peppered moth is pale-coloured and "peppered" with black speckles.

2 A **mutation** in the moth's **DNA** produces a slightly different version. It is darker, with lighter speckles.

3 In general, light-coloured moths produced light-coloured offspring. Dark-coloured moths passed their mutation on to their offspring.

4 During the day, the moths rest on tree trunks. Light-coloured moths blended in with the bark.

5 This camouflage made it harder for birds to see and eat the light-coloured moths. They lived longer and passed on their **genes**. In the early 1800s, the light-coloured moths were much more common than the dark-coloured ones.

7 The light-coloured moths were no longer well camouflaged. More and more were eaten by birds. The dark-coloured moths now blended in better. They were more likely to survive and pass on their genes.

6 Soon, coal-burning factories started spewing soot into the air. It settled on trees, making their trunks darker.

9 In the 1950s, new laws helped reduce air pollution. There was now less soot on the trees. The light-coloured moths had the better camouflage once more. They became more common again.

8 Over time, the dark-coloured moths became more common.

Earth is home to an amazing variety of animals, but it took a long time to get where we are today. When the planet first formed, about 4.5 billion years ago, it was a ball of hot rock surrounded by poisonous gases. It was also bombarded by a rain of **comets** and **meteors**. It wasn't the sort of place anyone would want to live!

LIFE BEGINS

About 3.8 billion years ago, life began on Earth. But if you think this means dinosaurs, think again! The first living things were tiny, single-celled microbes. It took another billion years at least before cells started to get more complex. And it wasn't until about 900 million years ago (mya) that living things made up of more than one cell appeared.

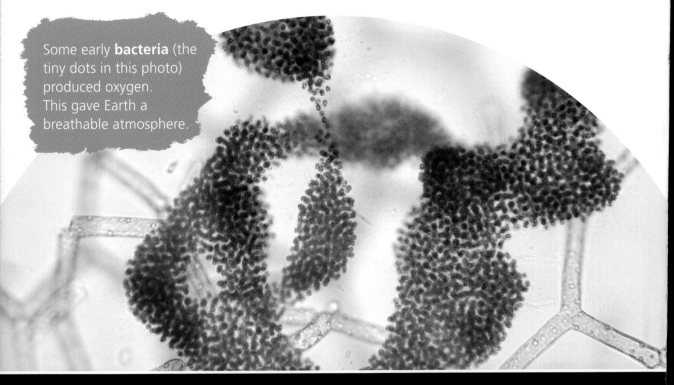

Some early **bacteria** (the tiny dots in this photo) produced oxygen. This gave Earth a breathable atmosphere.

The dinosaurs appeared at least 243 mya.

Weird and wonderful creatures soon **evolved**, colonizing the oceans and then the land. About 365 mya the first four-legged animals appeared: the ancestors of today's mammals, reptiles, birds and amphibians. Dinosaurs appeared about 230 mya, and for millions of years, they ruled the Earth. But an **asteroid** impact 66 mya wiped them out.

HAIRY FACT

The end of the dinosaurs was what's called a mass extinction, when huge numbers of **species** die out in a short period of time. Earth has gone through several mass extinctions. The Permian mass extinction (about 250 mya) wiped out 96 per cent of all species that existed! Everything living on Earth today is descended from the few species that survived.

A NEW WORLD

Many scientists believe that the asteroid impact changed Earth's **climate**. Plants died, and so did the animals that ate them – including the dinosaurs. But smaller, more adaptable animals were able to find food and survive. They became the ancestors of the species that we know today.

BRANCHING OFF

Today, the group known as **primates** includes apes, monkeys and lemurs. Their ancestors first appeared shortly after the dinosaurs died out. Over millions of years, they changed and became **adapted** to conditions in different **habitats**. One by one, distinct species branched off. Some developed into the monkeys that we see today. Others became great apes such as gorillas, orangutans – and us!

Even without mass extinctions, species still die out. The deinotherium became **extinct** about 2 mya, possibly due to climate change.

Humans are not descended from chimps. Chimps and humans share a **common ancestor**, making us more like distant cousins.

NEVER STOPPING

Evolution sometimes happens over a very long timeframe, so it can be hard to see its effects unless you look a long way back. We are so used to the animals and plants alive today that it's easy to forget that evolution is still happening. Earth's climate is changing, and living things must be adapted to the new conditions. Those that aren't will die out.

By the numbers

If you compressed (squashed) the entire history of Earth into a single 24-hour period, starting at midnight, the first life forms would appear at about 4.00 a.m. Land plants arrive about 18 hours later, and dinosaurs don't show up until 10.56 p.m. And humans? We're the real latecomers - we don't appear until just before one minute to midnight!

First life forms
4.00 a.m.

Land plants
10.00 p.m.

Dinosaurs
10.56 p.m.

Humans
11.59 p.m.

| 0.00 a.m. | 1.00 a.m. | 2.00 a.m. | 3.00 a.m. | 4.00 a.m. | 5.00 a.m. | 6.00 a.m. | 7.00 a.m. | 8.00 a.m. | 9.00 a.m. | 10.00 a.m. | 11.00 a.m. | 12.00 a.m. | 1.00 p.m. | 2.00 p.m. | 3.00 p.m. | 4.00 p.m. | 5.00 p.m. | 6.00 p.m. | 7.00 p.m. | 8.00 p.m. | 9.00 p.m. | 10.00 p.m. | 11.00 p.m. | 12.00 p.m. |

Over many thousands of years, evolution has shaped the animals that we know today. Animals live in a huge range of **habitats**. All of them have **adaptations** to make them better suited to their habitat.

SNOW LEOPARD

Snow leopards live in the cold, snowy mountains of central Asia, where the air is thin and cold. Their long, thick fur helps keep them warm. The spaces behind their nostrils are larger than normal. They warm up the cold air before it travels to the lungs. The snow leopard's large, muscular chest lets it take deep breaths, to get as much oxygen as possible.

LESSER FLAMINGO

Africa's soda lakes are dangerous places – the warm water is both salty and very **caustic**. It would be deadly for many creatures, but lesser flamingoes are at home there. Tough skin and scales protect their legs. When they drink the warm water, they can even filter out the salt! Most **predators** can't follow them into this dangerous habitat, so the flamingoes can feed in relative safety.

GALÁPAGOS LAND IGUANA

Galápagos land iguanas live on hot volcanic islands, where water is scarce. They are adapted to get the moisture they need from their food: mainly from cactuses, which store water in their fleshy stems. The iguanas dig burrows to escape the worst of the heat.

HOODED SEAL

Hooded seals live in the freezing Arctic, hunting for food in the icy waters. A thick layer of blubber protects them from the cold as they swim. Female seals produce incredibly rich milk for their babies. The babies only feed for four days, and they grow fast. They can swim at a very young age. This helps them escape the polar bears that hunt them.

ON THE MOVE

Animals are masters of movement. They walk, gallop, fly, glide, dive and swim through a range of habitats. Different adaptations have given them the bodies – and the skills – they need to get where they want to go.

SLOTH

Sloths are perfectly suited to life in rainforest trees. They hang upside down from branches using their long, curved claws. Their fur even grows pointing away from their hands and feet. This allows the rain to run off them when they're hanging upside down. By staying in the trees and moving slowly, sloths can avoid predators.

ALBATROSS

An albatross looks heavy and clumsy on the ground, but these large seabirds are masters of the air. Their long, **streamlined** wings let them soar for many kilometres with very little effort, looking for food. Other birds have to use their muscles to keep their wings extended. However, an albatross's shoulders have a special **tendon** to make things easier. It locks the wing in place when it is fully extended.

FLEA

Tiny fleas jump high to reach the animals they feed on. Their bodies have a pad of special protein that acts like a spring. They use their muscles to squeeze this "spring", storing energy in it. Then, when they are ready, they crouch and release the spring. As they push their feet into the ground, the jointed back legs act as levers to provide power. The flea's body launches into the air.

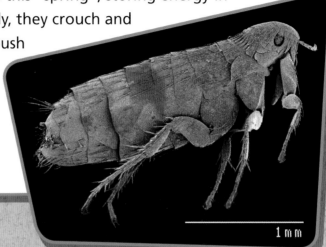

1 mm

SAILFISH

When it comes to speed in the water, it's hard to beat a sailfish. These speedy swimmers have strong, muscular bodies. The sailfish's sharp, pointed bill helps cut through the water, and a crescent-shaped tail helps provide speed.

HIDE AND SEEK

Any animal that doesn't want to be eaten needs a plan – such as hiding, or outrunning its predators. Even hunters need adaptations to give them the best chance of catching enough food to survive.

LEAF INSECT

Anyone looking for a nice juicy insect to eat isn't going to bother with a leaf – so that's what a leaf insect's body looks like! They spend most of their time on the plants that they eat, so they hide by blending in. They even take their disguise a step further by swaying as they walk. This makes them look like a leaf blowing in the wind.

PAINTED FROGFISH

It's easier to catch food when your prey comes to you! The painted frogfish is camouflaged to blend in with the background. But it has a special spine with a fleshy tip that looks like a small fish. When another sea creature comes closer to investigate … SNAP!

CHEETAH

The simplest way to catch food is to be faster than everyone else. The cheetah is a lean, mean running machine, capable of bursts of speed that leave other animals in the dust. They have a slender body, flexible spine, blunt claws and a powerful heart. These features combine to produce a long, bounding stride.

GECKO

Geckos have an unusual way of avoiding predators: when threatened, they can shed their entire tail! What's even weirder is that the shed tail continues to move for up to half an hour. This distracts the predator and lets the gecko escape. A gecko will eventually grow a new tail, though it may not look exactly like the original.

CHANGING BEHAVIOUR

Not all **adaptations** change the shape of an animal's body. Different behaviours can help an animal survive and communicate. Sometimes these behaviours are **inherited** from parents, and sometimes they are learned.

BAT

If you're going to hunt insects in the dark of night, your eyes aren't going to be much use. Bats get around this problem by using echolocation. They send out high-pitched sounds and listen to the echoes bouncing back. The time it takes for the echoes to come back tells them where objects are. Using echolocation, a bat can pinpoint prey as small as a mosquito.

BEE

Bees live in large groups, and they cooperate to find enough nectar for everyone. To do this, they need to be able to tell each other where the best sources of nectar are. The solution? A dance, of course! A bee performs a "waggle dance", which tells the other bees the direction, distance and richness of the nectar source.

NEW CALEDONIAN CROW

Humans use tools every day, but a few animals use them as well. Some **species** of crows use twigs to get at grubs hidden in wood. And they can be very picky about their tools! The crows will discard twigs that aren't good enough, and they will look after their favourite tools.

VERVET MONKEY

Many animals call out to warn other animals in their group about danger. Vervet monkeys take this a step further. They have different calls that let the other monkeys know what kind of **predator** is near. Just by listening to the danger call, a monkey can tell whether a leopard, eagle or snake is nearby.

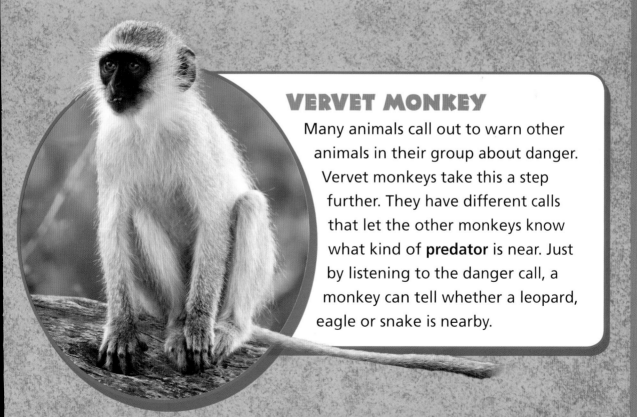

THE NEXT GENERATION

One of an animal's biggest responsibilities is producing the next generation. Their behaviour gives them a better chance of attracting a mate. It can also give their **offspring** the best possible chance of survival.

NATTERJACK TOAD

To produce offspring, an animal must first find a mate. The male natterjack toad does this by calling out. And it's not just any call! Their rasping, croaking "rrrrrrrrrRUP!" is made even louder by a special sac in the throat. The call can be heard up to 2 kilometres (1 mile) away.

BOWERBIRD

The male bowerbirds of Australia and Papua New Guinea know that they need to stand out if they want a mate. They build elaborate structures called bowers, using twigs, pebbles, fruit, flowers and other objects. They will even use broken glass and plastic lids. Then they stand in the bower and wait for a female to come and admire it.

EMPEROR PENGUIN

Parenting is a tough job, so it helps if both parents share the load. Emperor penguins breed during the freezing Antarctic winter, far from the coast where they find their food. The male keeps the egg warm while the female goes off to feed. When she returns, she takes over looking after the chick while the male goes to feed.

MEERKAT

Sometimes two parents aren't enough – extra help is needed. Meerkats live in groups where most of them are related. The top male and female have babies, but the mother's main priority is eating enough to produce milk for the babies. Other adults in the group step in to babysit while she looks for food. The "babysitters" teach the young and protect them from danger.

THE RISE OF THE HUMANS

Compared to the dinosaurs, humans are latecomers on Earth, but we still have a long history. Over millions of years, we have **evolved** from simple apes into modern creatures who can build, dance and invent.

OUT OF AFRICA

Long ago, a **species** of ape lived in Africa. It was probably hairy and walked on four legs. This ancient ape is our distant ancestor – and the ancestor of chimpanzees too. The population of apes eventually split into two separate groups (many scientists think this happened about 13 mya). One group developed into humans, and the other into chimpanzees. Chimpanzees will never evolve into humans; they are following a separate evolutionary path.

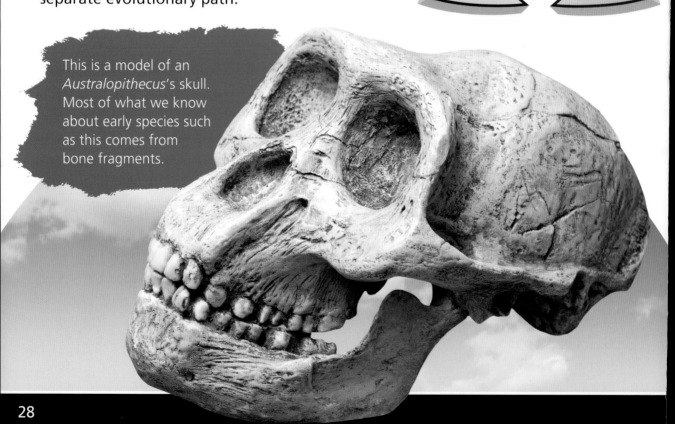

Chimpanzees

Humans

This is a model of an *Australopithecus*'s skull. Most of what we know about early species such as this comes from bone fragments.

WALKING UPRIGHT

By about 4 million years ago, the human branch had developed into a group of species known as *Australopithecus*. These apes had long, strong arms and fingers for climbing trees, but they could walk upright. There were some advantages to walking on two legs instead of four. For example, standing upright allows you to see farther. It also frees up your hands for holding or using tools.

Australopithecus looked very different to us, but you can still tell that we're related.

By the numbers

Adult *Australopithecus* males were, on average, 150 centimetres (4.9 feet) tall, which is about the size of a 12 year-old child. At 105 centimetres (3.4 feet), females were a lot shorter – more like a 5-year-old. Their brains were small too: usually less than 500 cubic centimetres. That is about one-third the size of a modern human brain.

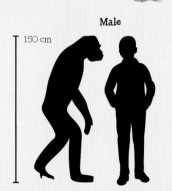

Male

150 cm

Female

105 cm

GETTING SMARTER

Australopithecus belonged to a family called **hominids**. It's a very big family which also includes gorillas, orangutans and chimps. About 2.5 million years ago, a new **genus** called *Homo* split off and began to develop separately. Never heard of it? Well, you should have – *Homo* is the genus that you belong to!

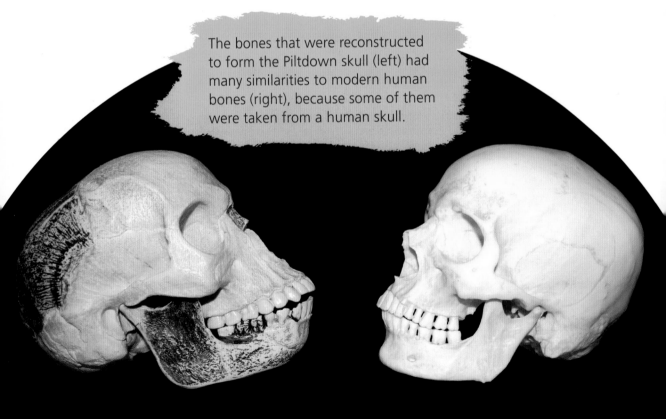

The bones that were reconstructed to form the Piltdown skull (left) had many similarities to modern human bones (right), because some of them were taken from a human skull.

TOOLMAKERS

One of the earliest members of the *Homo* genus was *Homo habilis*, which means "handy man". Like *Australopithecus*, it was short, with long arms. However, it had a bigger brain, and it put it to good use making stone tools. Scientists think that *Homo habilis* fed on meat from animals killed by other animals. They used stone tools to smash bones and get at the soft marrow inside.

Homo habilis walked upright and had a smaller jaw and more human-like teeth than *Australopithecus*.

WE ARE FAMILY ... OR ARE WE?

Two new species soon followed: *Homo ergaster* in Africa and *Homo erectus* in Asia. (Scientists can't agree whether these are actually separate species, or different versions of the same one.) *Homo ergaster* was tall and thin, shaped more like modern humans, and probably fairly hairless. *Homo erectus* was shorter and stockier. Both species used stone tools, and may have been able to use fire too.

HERE COME THE HUMANS!

About 600,000 years ago, a new species called *Homo heidelbergensis* appeared. They were tall and strong and lived in groups who worked together to hunt, using stone-tipped spears. But they didn't last. Before long, two new – and very familiar – species appeared.

CULTURED CAVEMEN

We use "neanderthal" as a word for a stupid, uncultured person, but this is unfair on *Homo neanderthalensis*. These hominids were stocky and muscular, with big brains. They made complex stone tools, built shelters and buried their dead. Neanderthals only died out about 28,000 years ago, and were our closest cousins. In fact, modern humans and Neanderthals sometimes had babies together!

Scientists use bones to recreate what Neanderthals' bodies would have looked like.

BETTER BRAINS, LESS HAIR

Modern humans – *Homo sapiens*, to give us our proper name – lived alongside Neanderthals for thousands of years. We have taller, slimmer bodies, with less hair. Although our brains are smaller, humans are more intelligent. (This may be because a larger portion of a Neanderthal's brain was devoted to sight and to controlling a larger body.) And we invented all sorts of things, from clothing and metal tools to cars and computers!

HAIRY FACT

Humans have some very bizarre relatives. An enormous ape called *Gigantopithecus* may have survived up to about 100,000 years ago. It stood 3 metres (9.8 feet) high and weighed up to 500 kilograms (1,102 pounds). At the other end of the scale, scientists recently discovered **fossils** of tiny human-like creatures, just 1 metre (3.3 feet) tall, in Indonesia. They are nicknamed "hobbits" because of their small size and large feet.

Gigantopithecus would have been alive at the same time as Neanderthals and modern humans.

Every human being is unique, but we still have a huge amount in common. There are some **adaptations** that set humans apart. Some are physical and some are behavioural, but all have come about thanks to the process of evolution.

Some scientists think that our smaller jaws and teeth may have made it easier to develop speech.

TAKING IT ON THE CHIN

Compared to our **hominid** relatives, human jaws and teeth are pretty small. Early hominids ate everything raw, and it took strong muscles and teeth to chew it. Humans, on the other hand, were able to use tools to slice or pound their food. This meant that it needed less chewing, so our jaws became smaller. These smaller jaws may have helped in the development of spoken language.

A WORLD OF COLOUR

Dogs, cats and most other mammals can only see certain colours of light – a bit like a person who is colour-blind. Humans and our closest relatives (including chimpanzees and orangutans) can see in brilliant colour. This is partly because we are active during the day, when colour vision is most useful.

Another possible reason is that our lack of body hair allows our emotions to show when our skin flushes. You need full-colour vision to see this, so evolution might have favoured individuals who could size up other people more easily.

Evolution in action

Some baby animals are able to walk around within hours of birth, but human babies are helpless. This may be because of our complex brains and behaviour. Our long period of childhood gives babies the time they need to learn language and other behaviours from their parents.

A child is constantly learning from its parents.

CULTURAL ADAPTATIONS

Most animal **species** are **adapted** to life in one particular **habitat**. Humans, on the other hand, can live just about anywhere. Our big brains can think up solutions to the problems posed by different habitats. In addition, the way we live and communicate allows us to share knowledge in a way that animals can't.

TALK, TALK, TALK

Animals communicate in various ways, but humans use complex spoken language. Many scientists think language developed over time as an adaptation that helped humans survive. Communicating with each other helped us work together to farm, hunt and adjust to different conditions. Other scientists think that our brains developed to make us better at making tools, and spoken language simply happened as a result of that.

The number of languages means that not all humans can understand each other.

SOCIAL ANIMALS

Human **culture** is incredibly complex. We have complicated relationships with family and friends. We have to learn cultural rules. We also learn the knowledge that our culture passes down over the generations. We write down ideas and create art and literature. This sharing of information gives humans an edge over other species.

By the numbers

It is estimated that there are at least 7,000 different languages in the world. Some are very widespread – about 900 million people speak Mandarin as a first language. On the other hand, some languages have just a few speakers. Papua New Guinea, with a population of about 7 million, has well over 800 languages!

WORLD POPULATION

POPULATION OF MANDARIN SPEAKERS

POPULATION OF PAPUA NEW GUINEA

School not only teaches children facts, but also how to work together and share knowledge.

A DIVERSE WORLD

You've probably noticed that not all humans look alike – the differences are hard to miss! People can be short and stocky, or tall and thin. Our skin and hair come in a variety of different colours, and our facial features are different too.

THE SKIN YOU'RE IN

Humans first appeared in hot places, which is one reason we have so little body hair. But humans' skin was damaged by sunlight. So evolution provided melanin – a brown **pigment** that acts as a natural sunscreen. People from the **tropics** generally have more melanin, giving them darker skin.

Melanin blocks **ultraviolet (UV) rays**, which can be harmful. But we need some UV rays to allow the body to produce vitamin D. When people moved to colder places with less sunlight, they developed lighter skin colour, to absorb enough UV rays.

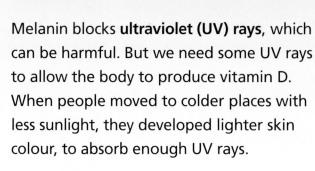

Hair colour is controlled by the same **pigments** as skin colour, and the amount of pigment you have is all down to your genes.

UNIQUE FACES

Human faces show great variety. Although we all have the same basic features, they can be shaped or aligned differently. Unique faces aren't as important to animals who use smell or sound to identify each other. But for humans, who use their sight instead, there is a real advantage to being able to recognize faces – and to being easily recognizable.

Evolution in action

Scientists studied Neanderthal **fossils** and discovered that some of them may have had ginger hair and freckles, just like humans. The **gene** that causes ginger hair also causes pale skin. This helps people in areas with less sun to get enough vitamin D.

ALL SHAPES AND SIZES

The shape of a person's body is affected by factors such as diet and exercise. But evolution has also played a role in shaping our bodies. For example, round bodies and narrow noses stop heat escaping. Early humans with these features had a better chance of surviving in cold **climates**. In hot areas, it was better to have a tall, thin body.

Groups of humans have thrived in many different climates.

By the numbers

The Dutch are the tallest nation in the world, with an average height of just over 183 cm (6 feet) for men, and 170 cm (5 feet 7 inches) for women. The average height in the Netherlands has shot up enormously over the past 150 years. Some people think this is due to the dairy-rich diet there. Other studies have shown that taller men have more children, passing on their tall genes.

183 cm

170 cm

BLOOD GROUPS

Human blood comes in different groups, called A, B, AB and O, and each of these groups can be either positive or negative. Your blood group is determined by genes passed on by your parents. Some blood groups are more common in certain parts of the world. However, scientists still can't agree on why these different groups **evolved**, or what purpose they serve.

If a person needs a blood transfusion, doctors have to make sure they use the right blood group.

MIXING TOGETHER

For thousands of years, different peoples tended to marry and have children within their own group. This meant that certain physical and cultural **traits** were often associated with particular groups. Today, people are mixing as never before. Genes are being spread around the world. This makes us more adaptable as a **species**.

HUMANS OF THE FUTURE

Evolution is an ongoing process, and that applies to humans too! In the future, we may look very different. The **traits** that made individuals successful back when we hunted with spears are not the same ones that make people successful today. Over a long period of time, our modern lives will favour certain traits. We also use technology to stop **natural selection** from happening.

Technology may have a bigger effect on future humans than the environment.

Evolution in action

Some changes in our bodies happen fast. Smartphones have not been around for long, but they may already be changing the way our brains work. Studies suggest that heavy technology users are better at multi-tasking, although the trade-off may be a shorter attention span.

VISIBLE CHANGES

Many people have wondered about possible changes to our appearance. Our constant use of screens may affect the way our eyes process light. This may mean bigger eyes – and the whites of our eyes might possibly become red. More time spent sitting down may lead to bigger bottoms and a more rounded spine. More exposure to **ultraviolet (UV) rays** – due to thinning of the ozone layer – may lead to darker skin.

AGE OF TECHNOLOGY

Some changes may not be down to evolution. We are learning how to use technology to change the human body. Doctors can transplant body parts. They can replace missing limbs with artificial ones called prosthetics. Thanks to technology, humans of the future may not age quickly – or show any signs of ageing at all! We might be able to upgrade our eyes, or use tiny robots to repair our bodies from the inside. The possibilities are endless!

WHAT IF HUMANS HAD NOT EVOLVED?

Think about what you have learned so far about evolution and human history. Over the years, our **species** has been shaped by our **genes** and our environment. But what if we had not **evolved**?

THINK ABOUT IT!

What if, for instance, we still walked on four legs or were covered in hair? How do you think this might change the way we live? For example, if we still had furry bodies, we wouldn't need clothes to keep warm. We might also find it harder to recognize other humans if their features were covered in hair. This may have led us to develop other ways to recognize each other, such as a better sense of smell.

SUPER-HUMAN

Think about what **adaptations** might be best in today's world. What **traits** could help a person survive and succeed in modern life? Can you think of any traits or abilities that humans don't yet have, which might be useful today? Draw a picture of what you think this super-human would look like.

Big head to keep all the knowledge in

Device implanted in hand

Wheels as feet to get around quicker

Technology to allow us to control objects with our minds

Bigger eyes from looking at screens

Special glowing clothes to see in the dark

Hologram palm

Extra-long finger from constantly texting

Gadget belt

Rocket feet

TIMELINE OF HUMAN EVOLUTION

55 mya	The first **primates evolve**.
14 mya	The first gorillas branch off from the primate family tree.
13 mya	Chimpanzees branch off from the primate family tree.
4 mya	*Australopithecus* first appears, with a small brain but walking upright on two legs.
2.5 mya	First appearance of *Homo habilis*, which has a slightly larger brain and begins to make and use stone tools.
2 mya	*Homo ergaster* appears in Africa.
1.8 mya	In Asia, **fossils** of *Homo erectus* are found from this period. Their brains are larger than those of *Homo ergaster*. They may be a different version of *Homo ergaster*, or a completely separate **species**.
1.6 mya	**Hominids** may have started to use fire around this time, but it may not have been widespread until much later.
600,000 years ago	*Homo heidelbergensis*, a large-brained hominid, lives in Africa and Europe.

500,000 years ago	The first purpose-built shelters found so far date from this period.
400,000 years ago	Hominids begin to hunt with stone-tipped spears.
400,000 years ago	Neanderthals appear and are found across Europe.
200,000 years ago	*Homo sapiens* appears and journeys through Asia and Europe.
150,000 years ago	Humans become capable of speech.
50,000 years ago	Humans reach Australia.
33,000 years ago	The oldest known cave art dates from this period.
28,000 years ago	Neanderthals become **extinct**.
about 16,000 years ago	Humans from Asia reach the Americas.
10,000 years ago	Humans first begin to farm and settle in villages.

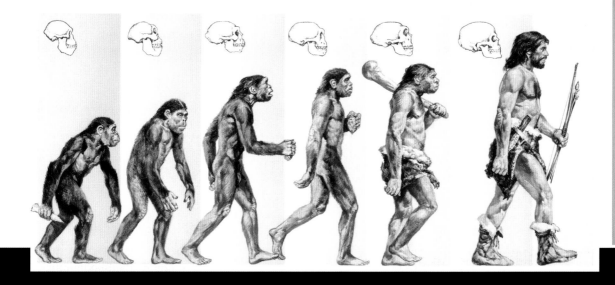

GLOSSARY

adapt change in order to survive; a change in an animal or plant is called an adaptation

adaptation *see* **adapt**

asteroid large space rock that moves around the sun

bacteria one-celled, microscopic living things that exist all around you and inside you

caustic able to destroy or eat away by chemical action

cell smallest unit of a living thing

chromosome thread-like structure in a cell that carries the genes

climate usual weather that occurs in a place

comet ball of rock and ice that circles the sun

common ancestor most recent form or species from which two different species are both descended

culture customs, beliefs and way of life of a particular group of people

DNA (short for deoxyribonucleic acid) molecule that carries all of the instructions to make a living thing and keep it working

evolve to change gradually, especially animals or plants

extinct no longer living; an extinct animal is one that has died out, with no more of its kind

fossil remains or traces of plants and animals that are preserved as rock

gene part of every cell that carries physical and behavioural information passed from parents to their children

genus classification grouping that includes a number of different, but closely related, species of plants or animals

habitat natural place and conditions in which a plant or animal lives

hominid any member of the family of two-legged primates that includes all humans and their ancestors

inherited receive a physical characteristic or behaviour from parents

meteor piece of rock or dust that enters Earth's atmosphere, causing a streak of light in the sky

molecule smallest part of a substance that can exist and still keep the characteristics of the substance

mutation change from the original gene

naturalist person who studies the natural world, especially plants and animals

natural selection natural process of evolution in which the organisms that are best adapted to their environment survive and reproduce, while those that are weak leave fewer or no offspring

offspring the young of a person, animal or plant

organism living thing such as a plant, animal, bacterium or fungus

pigment substance that gives something its particular colour

predator animal that hunts other animals for food

primate animal in the group of mammals that include humans, apes and monkeys

species group of living things with similar features that can mate with each other but not with those of other groups

streamlined shaped to move efficiently through the air or water

tendon strong band of tissue that attaches a muscle to a bone

trait quality or characteristic that makes one person or animal different from another

tropics warm region of Earth that is near the equator

ultraviolet (UV) rays

variation something that is slightly different from another thing of the same type

BOOKS

All About Evolution (Big Questions), Robert Winston (Dorling Kindersley, 2016)

Evolution (Science Sorted), Glenn Murphy (Macmillan Children's Books, 2014)

The Evolution of You and Me (Planet Earth), Michael Bright (Wayland, 2016)

The Rise of the Mammals (Evolution), Matthew Rake (Hungry Tomato, 2015)

What Is Evolution?, Louise Spilsbury (Wayland, 2016)

WEBSITES

This fantastic site has a huge range of examples of different animal adaptations:
www.bbc.co.uk/nature/adaptations

Go here for a more detailed breakdown of Darwin's theory:
**www.bbc.co.uk/schools/gcsebitesize/science/21c_pre_2011/evolution/
theoryevolutionrev2.shtml**

Visit this site to find out more about *Australopithecus*:
www.dkfindout.com/uk/history/stone-age/human-ancestors

Use this interactive family tree to find out more about humans and our ancestors:
humanorigins.si.edu/evidence/human-family-tree

PLACES TO VISIT

National Museum of Scotland
Chambers Street
Edinburgh
EH1 1JF
**www.nms.ac.uk/national-
museum-of-scotland**

Natural History Museum
Cromwell Road
London
SW7 5BD
www.nhm.ac.uk

Oxford University Museum of
Natural History
Parks Road
Oxford
OX1 3PW
www.oum.ox.ac.uk

INDEX